ECOLOGY AN_
THE ENVIRONMENT

STEP-BY-STEP

English edition first published in Australia and New Zealand in 2009 by Gecko Press
PO Box 9335, Marion Square, Wellington 6141, New Zealand
Email: info@geckopress.com

National Library of New Zealand Cataloguing-in-Publication Data

Michel, François.
L'ecologie à petits pas
Ecology and the environment / text by François Michel ; illustrated by Marc Boutavant.
(Step-by-step)
ISBN 978-1-877467-29-5
1. Ecology—Juvenile literature. [1. Ecology.] I. Title. II. Boutavant, Marc.
III. Series: Step-by-step (Gecko Press)
577—dc 22

Translated by Jean Anderson
Edited by Raymond Huber
Designed by Archetype, New Zealand
Printed by Everbest, China

ISBN: 978-1-877467-29-5

For more curiously good books, please visit www.geckopress.com

ECOLOGY AND THE ENVIRONMENT

STEP-BY-STEP

François Michel

Illustrations by Marc Boutavant

GECKO PRESS

Contents

What is your environment? 4

The environment in danger 6

What is ecology? 8

Ecosystems 10

Life from the soil 12

Who eats what? 14

The water cycle 16

What's in the atmosphere? 18

Deadly pollution 22

Water, water everywhere … 24

Hands off my water! 28

Let's clean up our water 32

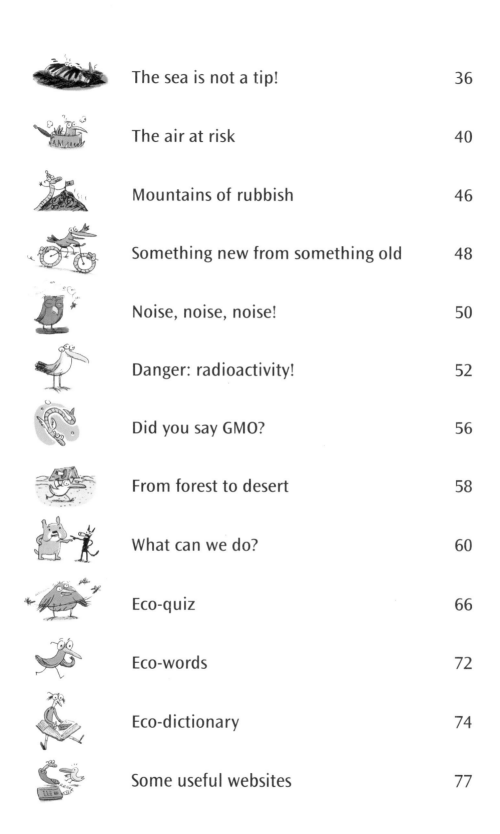

The sea is not a tip!   36

The air at risk   40

Mountains of rubbish   46

Something new from something old   48

Noise, noise, noise!   50

Danger: radioactivity!   52

Did you say GMO?   56

From forest to desert   58

What can we do?   60

Eco-quiz   66

Eco-words   72

Eco-dictionary   74

Some useful websites   77

What is your environment?

Your environment is what is all around you – your surroundings. Wherever you live, there's an environment to discover. It may be a city, with its sounds and streets, its buildings, factories and gardens. Or the countryside, with mountains, rivers and beaches, farms and forests.

To see your environment, find a high point such as the top of a building or hill. Turn slowly in a full circle, and observe your surroundings. Binoculars help you see even more.

How would you describe your environment? Is it a city or a town; a block of flats or a house? Is it quiet or noisy; flat or hilly; coastal or inland?

The environment in danger

When you look closely at your surroundings you'll notice all the changes humans have made to the natural environment. Over the last 150 years, industry, housing and farming have changed it more than any time in our whole history.

The earth is in danger! Human activities use up a lot of water and energy. We also make vast amounts of waste – which ends up in the air, the soil and the water. What kind of planet are we creating for the people of the future?

Intensive farming

Single crop farming, pesticides

Mining and quarrying

Dams and canals

Industry growing

Population growing

Transport networks spreading

What is ecology?

The word 'ecology' comes from two Greek words: *oikos*, meaning house or habitat, and *logia*, which means 'study of'. Ecology is knowing about how living things are connected to the surroundings (habitat) they live in. A habitat can be a natural or developed place.

The science of ecology started in the 19th century when Charles Darwin began his theory of evolution. Other scientists showed how important the soil and water were as habitats for living creatures.

Air and water are the two elements which living things need to grow. There is air and water flowing around your body, as well as through the soil, rivers, cities, sky and ocean. Everything is connected to everything else.

Cycles are an important part of ecology. Cycles make the natural world go around. There's the water cycle, the food cycle, the carbon cycle, the cycle of the seasons, and many others. If humans change these cycles too much, it can disturb every kind of life on Earth.

9

Ecosystems

An ecosystem is an area that has developed all by itself on Earth, because of the climate. Forests, lakes, wetlands and grasslands are all ecosystems. Each one has a special relationship with the plants and animals that live there. Ecosystems are often fragile places which can be disturbed by human activity.

The forest is home to a huge number of living things, especially in the hot, humid areas of the world. Life in a forest is organised in layers. On top are the leafy branches (the canopy), then the undergrowth, and the soil below. Each level has very different plants and animals. The biggest forests on Earth are in Northern Canada, Siberia and the Amazon.

Lakes, wetlands and swamps are also home to a vast range of living things.

Many creatures live their whole lives here, while others visit just to have their babies. A great number of animals come to drink and feed here. These watery spots are resting stages for birds that migrate long distances.

A large part of the planet is covered in natural grasslands where many different things live. Grasslands are also known as savannahs, steppes, tundras, pampas and pastures.

Life from the soil

The thin surface layer of our planet is called the soil. It's mostly made of earth (written with a small 'e') in which plants grow. This is the earth used by farmers and gardeners. It is made up of grains of sand and rock, a little clay, dead leaves and decaying creatures. There is water in it, too, and a great variety of life forms — animals, insects, microbes and fungi.

Plants anchor themselves in the soil with their roots. They can actually make their own food.

Plants draw the water and minerals they need from the earth. From these they make sap, which rises into the leaves. The leaves breathe in carbon dioxide (CO_2) from the air – and they use the energy of sunlight to change the CO_2 into food for themselves. And most amazing of all is that the leaves breathe out oxygen – a gas which we could not live without.

Thank you so much, plants! You create food we can eat and air we can breathe.

Who eats what?

To live and grow, every living thing has to eat another life form, plant or animal. This is called the food chain (or food cycle) and we are a part of it. If a link in this chain is broken or poisoned, everything in the chain is affected.

Every food chain begins with a kind of plant. It may be the size of a tree or only seen through a microscope, such as plankton.

An owl eats a sparrow that ate an insect that swallowed an aphid that sucked the sap from a tree. A shark eats a tuna fish that swallowed a sardine that fed on plankton. A hyena feeds on the body of a lion that ate a gazelle that grazed on the leaves of a bush. It's the cycle of life.

Some creatures are herbivores (vegetarians), while others are carnivores (meat eaters), or omnivores that eat pretty much everything.

If there were no plants there would be no food, so there would be no animals, and no humans on planet Earth.

The water cycle

Water is the secret of life — Earth's liquid miracle. This is the only planet in the solar system where water can be found in all of its three forms. Water can be a solid (ice), a liquid (water) and a gas (vapour). Water dissolves nearly everything and transports everything. But water can also become a raging demon, when rivers suddenly flood and destroy, or are polluted with terrible diseases.

Let's look at the water cycle — one of the major cycles on the earth's surface.

Water evaporates from the surface of seas, rivers and lakes, and from the soil following rainfall.

Plants also release a lot of water vapour into the air. This is called evapotranspiration.

Clouds contain water: as water vapour, water droplets or ice crystals (it depends on the season and the height of the clouds).

The wind blows the clouds across the sea and the land.

When it rains or snows, this is called precipitation.

Water seeps down into the soil, then comes back to the surface through springs.

Water runs along the surface of the earth as creeks, streams and rivers.

The water from rivers returns to the sea at river mouths or estuaries.

What's in the atmosphere?

The atmosphere is an envelope of gases that surrounds Earth.
It's hundreds of kilometres deep, but the atmosphere we can live
in is only a few kilometres thick. At the top of Mount Everest
(at 8,848 metres), it is almost impossible for people to breathe.

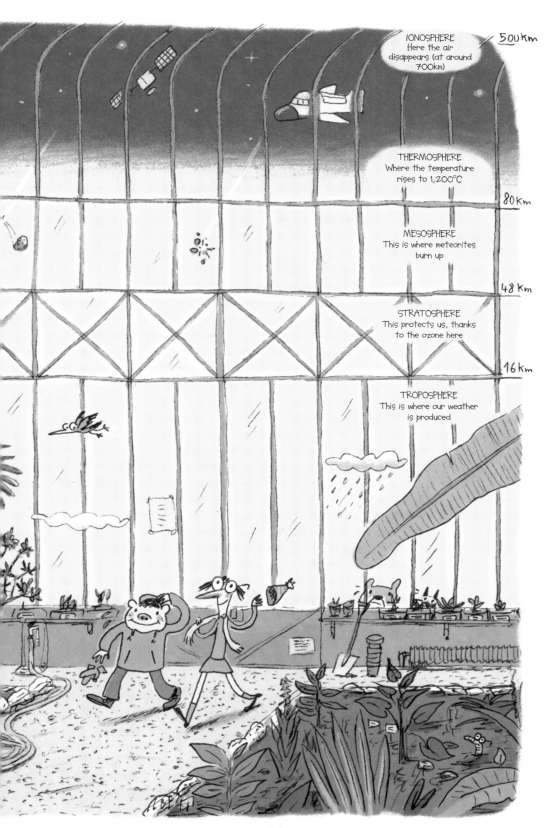

19

The atmosphere plays a lot of different roles. It allows living creatures to breathe and plants to feed. It also protects us against the sun's rays, warms the earth and allows the water cycle to be completed.

The air we breathe is a compound of all the gases that make up the atmosphere. It is made up of nitrogen (78%), oxygen (21%) and other gases (1%), such as carbon dioxide.

Ozone is a gas found in a very thin layer at about 30 to 40 kilometres high.

The ozone layer protects Earth from the sun's ultraviolet rays. Without it, everything on the surface of the planet would be burned.

The atmosphere holds warmth in around Earth because it contains CO_2, water vapour and other gases. This is called the greenhouse effect. Without the greenhouse effect, the average temperature would be about $-18°C$ on the earth's surface, instead of about $+14°C$ as it is now. But if the amount of greenhouse gases increases, the temperature rises and the climate changes.

Deadly pollution

Pollution is a change to a habitat which upsets the balance of life. It is a danger to the health of living things and their population numbers. Pollution usually happens when toxic substances are present in a high concentration, or there are disease-carrying micro-organisms.

If you throw left-over paint into a corner of your garden or a stream, it will kill animals, plants and micro-organisms in the soil and water.

If you burn a plastic bag or a tyre, it gives off dangerous smoke.

And we drink the water!   And we breathe the air!   And we eat the plants and animals!

Some farm chemicals can pollute our food through the food chain. The insecticide DDT has now been banned but unfortunately it stays in the soil for a long time. From the soil, the DDT goes into plants, then into animals who eat the plants. Finally it passes to humans who eat the animals or plants.

How does the air get polluted? By the fumes from the exhaust pipes on all the cars driving every day along all the roads on the planet – plus all the fumes from all the factory and house chimneys.

Water is polluted by all the soapy water from washing, all the waste water from drains, all the factory outfall pipes, the fertilisers, the oil spills, and all the boat engines. In many places, the soil is also polluted because people don't always care what they dump in the environment.

Water, water everywhere…

There is a lot of water on Earth, but only a tiny amount of it is easily used. The rest is salty (97%), frozen or buried deep under the earth's surface.

Having water is one thing, but it needs to be safe to drink. More than a billion people on the planet do not have clean water each day. That's one in every five humans.

The amount of water each person uses each day varies a lot from country to country. In Ghana (Africa), people use 70 times less water than Europeans do, and 150 times less than North Americans, who use an average of 300 litres per day.

In some areas people have only a few litres a day. Water is in short supply in the north of Africa and in the Middle East, and their populations are growing rapidly.

Every year, 250 million people suffer from diseases linked to water, causing around ten million deaths.

It takes this much water to make the following products:

1 car: 35,000 litres

1 kg of paper: 300 litres

1 kg maize: 900 litres

1 kg of aluminium: 1,250 litres

1 kg of cheese: 1,100 litres

1 kg of wool: 150 litres

1 kg of sugar: 80 litres

1 kg of lettuce: 25 litres

It takes about this much water for these household events:

1 tap running for 3 minutes – 18 litres

1 tap dripping for 1 day – 200 litres

1 load of washing – 70 litres

1 shower – 30 litres

1 flush of the toilet – 8 litres

1 bath – 100 litres

1 dishwasher load – 20 litres

1 carwash – 200 litres

In cities that are growing quickly it is difficult to find water for everyone.

Water can be a cause of conflict and even war, particularly between countries which don't have a good supply. Sometimes water reserves – rivers, lakes and underground reservoirs – are shared with neighbouring countries. Access to clean water is one of the most important issues of our time.

Hands off my water!

Water has one really important feature — it can dissolve a large number of substances. This means it is easily polluted, which can be a very serious problem in some countries.

The waste water from every one of our homes contains many polluting substances: toilet waste, soap, detergents and other chemicals.

Manufacturing is an important cause of water pollution. Many factories produce waste chemicals such as acids and heavy metals. These are highly toxic and poison the water. However, modern factories do not pollute as much as factories did in the old days.

Many farmers use large amounts of chemical fertilisers and pesticides. These seep into the soil when it rains or when paddocks are watered. The chemicals pollute the underground water supplies, and are then passed on into the rivers and the oceans.

To prevent further contamination of waterways, there are a number of measures farmers can take. For example, special chemicals (nitrification inhibitors) can reduce loss of nitrogen from the soil, helping stop pollution of water supplies.

Pesticides kill pest insects – but they also kill creatures that humans need to survive, such as earthworms and pollinating insects. Birds and small mammals can also be harmed. Pesticides can pollute the water that is used to supply towns and cities.

If people dump rubbish in the wrong place, it can pollute the water. Rainwater runs through the trash and dissolves many substances which pollute the water in the ground below. This makes it impossible to pump water from there for drinking.

Today more than half of the world's major rivers are badly polluted. The pollution is likely to get worse unless there are restrictions on waste and unless more water treatment stations are built.

Large amounts of chemicals called phosphates and nitrates come from washing water, fertilisers and animal waste. These chemicals boost the growth of algae and other water plants, which then invade the waterways and make some animals disappear. This is called eutrophication.

Pollution in river and lake water can be found by chemical testing but also by noticing the presence of certain creatures (called bio-indicators). If there are trout and insect larvae present, the water is probably clean. But certain kinds of worms are signs that the water is polluted.

In the countryside, the removal of trees and the development of very large areas of farmland can encourage land-slips, soil erosion and even disastrous flooding.

Let's clean up our water

There are two ways to tackle the problem of water pollution. First, we must pollute less, and second, we must clean up our dirty water.

There are many ways to pollute less. Try using less detergent (or eco-friendly detergent) when washing your clothes and dishes. Don't ever pour toxic chemicals down the drain. Farmers can use less fertiliser and pesticide on paddocks, and not overwork the land.

A water treatment station is a kind of factory where the dirty water from a city is cleaned up. Then it can be returned to the waterways and re-join the water cycle. You can go and visit your city's water treatment plant. In some places, there are no proper treatment stations.

Sewers are drainpipes which run under a city or town. They collect the waste water from houses and factories. There's another kind of waste pipe called a stormwater drain. It collects rainwater running off streets. This water is not cleaned in a treatment station, so it's important to keep rubbish off the streets.

How waste water is cleaned

❶ Screening

The dirty water passes through several filters which separate out any large objects, paper, leaves and so on.

❹ Biological treatment

Bacteria feed on the organic part of the waste water.

❺ Clarification

Bacteria are separated from the clean water which can now be pumped back into rivers, lakes or the ocean.

❷ Separation

Solids are separated. Fat floats because it's lighter than water. Sand sinks to the bottom because it's heavier. Solids are then removed.

❸ Decanting

The water is left to rest for three to four hours. Over half the remaining dirt sinks to the bottom.

The sea is not a tip!

There are ports, large cities and many factories on the coast. Their sewers and stormwater drains often empty directly into the sea.

Coasts are also polluted from rivers and the millions of people who like to holiday at the beach.

Sometimes beaches are invaded by masses of green algae. The over-growth of algae is caused by too much phosphate and nitrate in the water. These chemicals come mainly from detergents and fertilisers.

Scientists can check the quality of our coastal waters. When there is too much pollution, the gathering and eating of shellfish is banned.

The Mediterranean Sea is almost entirely enclosed and can get very polluted. The worst areas are along the French and Italian beaches, and the Greek coast near Athens.

One sea is even disappearing! The Aral Sea in northern Uzbekistan has shrunk to half its size in 50 years. Why? Because the rivers that flow into it have been redirected to irrigate crops such as cotton.

Coral reefs are dying in some areas. Coral is actually a kind of animal and it is very sensitive to pollution and temperature rises. The beautiful Great Barrier Reef off the coast of Australia, and other Pacific reefs, are in danger of disappearing.

Oil spills are enormous expanses of oil that float on the surface of the sea. They can also wash onto beaches. Spills are caused by accidents and also by the tankers pumping oil out into the ocean. Oil has a deadly effect on plankton, seaweed, shellfish and seabirds which get covered in the sticky mess.

# The air at risk

Car and truck exhausts, plane engines, factory smoke, the burning of rubbish, gases from spray-cans and refrigerators — these are all things which can pollute the air we breathe.

Athens, Los Angeles, London, Sydney and Christchurch — many cities are often covered by a cloud of pollution. This dirty air can cause breathing diseases, nerve damage and even cancer.

Stone statues and monuments are damaged by acid pollution in the air. It changes limestone into gypsum, which wears away very quickly.

The air and the rain can become acidic. This is caused by sulphur dioxide which comes mainly from burning coal. 'Acid rain' can kill many trees and sometimes whole forests.

Big forest fires and explosive volcanic eruptions send huge amounts of gas into the atmosphere, which makes even more air pollution.

In many countries air quality is improving, because filters have been fitted to factory chimneys. But this is very expensive and not all factories are up to the cleanest air standard. Air pollution is increasing in many developing countries which don't yet have the technology for reducing pollution.

Carbon monoxide is a very dangerous gas which is produced by inefficient burning in heaters, cookers or motors. The gas joins on to red cells in the blood, stopping them from transporting oxygen and restricting breathing. Death can quickly follow. Gas and charcoal cookers should always be used where there is good flow of fresh air.

Asbestos is a dangerous product that should be avoided. It has very fine fibres which are used for insulating and are also fire-resistant. It has been used in buildings and to make fabrics. Asbestos fibres can be breathed into the lungs and cause serious health problems. It has been banned in many countries.

Cars pollute the air. Watch a car starting up when the exhaust is over a pile of fresh snow: the snow gets dirty in just a few seconds. New car models are fitted with converters to reduce pollution. Their engines run on lead-free petrol and give off lower amounts of dangerous gases – although still just as much CO_2 gas.

Scientists check the air quality in large cities. When the pollution levels are too high, drivers are asked to slow down. Some cities reduce the number of vehicles by allowing the use of cars with number plates ending in odd numbers one day, and even numbers the next day. But that's still not enough.

The greenhouse effect

Carbon dioxide (CO_2) is a very important gas. Green plants use it to make food, and it keeps the earth warm through the greenhouse effect. If the amount of carbon dioxide rises too much, temperatures will rise on the planet. Then the climate will change and large parts of the polar ice caps are at risk of melting. Scientists think that sea levels may rise by 50 cms or more by the year 2100. They have also worked out that if all the polar ice melted, the sea level would be 60 metres higher than it is today. Half the land would be under water.

Where does CO_2 come from? From everything that burns: wood in a fireplace, coal in a power station, petrol in an engine, and even from food in our bodies. We actually breathe out CO_2.

A hole in the ozone layer

Some gases are very harmful to the ozone layer. They come from aerosol cans, refrigerators, air-conditioners and insulation systems. These gases rise slowly into the atmosphere and gradually destroy the ozone layer. This is bad news, because ozone protects us from the sun's ultraviolet rays which burn our skin.

Since 1985, scientists have been monitoring the ozone layer. They've noticed that a hole forms every winter above the South Pole. The hole is growing larger every year, and the ozone layer is also getting thinner around the whole earth.

Although ozone is vital in the upper atmosphere, it is in fact a toxic and polluting gas down here on Earth. It is created by vehicle exhaust gases and factory emissions.

 # Mountains of rubbish

Big cities produce mountains of trash. This rubbish can take years to decompose (break down). Plastic bags and tin cans take hundreds of years to decompose, and aluminium cans up to 500 years. Worse still, plastic bottles may take a million years.

What's in the bin?

Various – 8%

Plastics – 10%

Metals – 5%

Glass – 14%

Dust – 8%

Paper and cardboard – 30%

Organic waste (food) – 25%

Highly toxic waste must not be put into the rubbish bin. Batteries and left-over paint or solvents must be placed in special containers.

Ask your city council where to find these containers.

46

Our rubbish is usually picked up from outside our houses. Where does it all go? Some of it is burned in incinerators. Cities can use this warmth to heat apartment buildings. The unburned part is sorted: metals are re-used, and the ashes can be used as a base for making roads.

A lot of waste still goes to the tip, which is an eyesore. It also pollutes the water underground unless the tip has been fitted with a waterproof liner.

As waste breaks down it gives off methane, which is another greenhouse gas.

The only real solution is to produce less waste. Several layers of paper and cardboard are used for a box of chocolates – is that really necessary?

Many of the products we throw away can be reused or recycled.

Something new from something old

Over 65% of the contents of our rubbish bins can be reused or recycled: paper, glass, plastics, metals and food. Organic (food) scraps can be made into compost which is great for the garden.

Before recycling waste, it must be sorted. Some cities have special rubbish collections with separate bins for glass, paper and organic waste. In other cities you have to take your rubbish to the containers set up in each neighbourhood, or to the tip.

By sorting and recycling, we reduce the amount of waste to be burned.

With recycled plastic we can make polar fleece, pipes, seats for public parks or garden sheds.

Glass is easy to recycle. It is simply broken up, melted down and used to make new products.

Scrap-metal dealers collect old metal. It's valuable for industrial use. For example, iron is melted down and reused to make corrugated iron and iron bars.

To recycle paper, the ink must first be removed from the old paper. Then it's pulped and transformed into newsprint, paper bags, cardboard and toilet paper.

Some artists create their sculptures and pictures from recycled materials or objects.

Noise, noise, noise!

Sledgehammers, motorbikes, horns, sirens, loud music, chainsaws, a motorway... noise is all around us, especially in a city. It is a kind of pollution in our environment and has a strong influence on our behaviour and our health.

Decibel levels of particular sounds:

Noise is measured in decibels (dB). Above 50 dB, a noise becomes irritating; above 90 dB, it is dangerous to our health.

Sometimes you can clearly hear the music from the headphones of a person's music player. These players can make a person deaf if the music is too loud.

Some of the risks connected with noise are gradual deafness, becoming irritable, losing concentration, tiredness and disturbed sleep.

Danger: radioactivity!

Radioactivity occurs in the natural world. Atoms (the building blocks of all matter) give off rays which are dangerous to varying degrees. You can't see or smell radioactivity. But it can be measured by devices such as Geiger counters.

Radioactivity is all around us, although at very low levels. Granite is a common rock that contains natural radioactivity. Like most pollution, the danger comes when there is an increase in radioactivity. The rays can cause blood diseases and digestive problems, burns, birth defects, cancers and even death.

When a nuclear bomb explodes, the heat and radiation are so strong they destroy everything within range. This happened when the USA dropped a bomb on Hiroshima, Japan, in 1945. Thirty thousand people died within a second and tens of thousands more died over the following days and years. Many people are still being treated today because they were exposed to radiation from this nuclear blast.

A nuclear power station uses a 'controlled' nuclear blast to make electricity. But a poorly-maintained station can be very dangerous. In Chernobyl, Russia, in 1986, a nuclear station exploded, due to human error and poor design. The following day a radioactive cloud stretched across the whole of Europe. Its traces can still be found within the ice on mountains. The radiation killed dozens of people nearby. Even today there are high levels of cancer in the population and serious birth defects in babies.

Nuclear power produces radioactive waste. But the radioactivity of a substance can last for several thousand years – this is called its hazardous life. For many years, large amounts of radioactive waste was buried or thrown away, especially into the sea.

Today, waste with a short hazardous life is placed in metal barrels, sometimes covered in concrete and then stored in dump sites. Waste with a long hazardous life is sealed and buried in concrete pits.

The advantage of nuclear power is that it produces electricity without burning oil or coal. This makes it much less polluting. But there are very high risks to weigh up, resulting from mechanical fault, a leak or an explosion. And of course nobody yet knows how to get rid of nuclear waste in the long term. However, many countries think the advantages outweigh the risks. For example, France gets 75% of its energy from nuclear power.

Did you say GMO?

The letters GMO stand for Genetically Modified Organism.
Think of all the features of living beings: the colour of your eyes,
the shape of a horse's legs, or the texture of the bark on a tree.
Everything that makes up a life form is programmed into the genes which
are passed on from generation to generation through the offspring.

Today, scientists are able to work with genes (this is called genetics). It's a marvellous
thing, because this could allow them to cure or prevent serious diseases or birth defects.
The advances of genetic science enable us to produce substances for medicines, such as
hormones, vitamins and vaccines.

Genetic science has produced new varieties of plants with special features. Some plants can grow faster, others are resistant to certain diseases or pesticides, while some just taste different. For example, some tomatoes have been created which almost never rot.

But there's a bit of a problem! We don't know how these GMOs will change over time, or even if they will reproduce naturally. Also, it has been noticed that certain GMO vegetables were harmful to pollinating insects such as bees. Without these insects many plants would not be able to reproduce.

Do GMO products have an effect on our health? There are very few answers. Many scientists believe we must be careful about putting GMOs into large scale use, something which has not yet been proven to be really necessary.

From forest to desert

Forests are environments which are especially important in keeping nature in balance on our planet. They are home to half the animal and plant species on Earth.

In recent years, tropical forests have come under very serious threat. Removal of forests can mean the land becomes like a desert. Forests also suffer from widespread damage due to fires, acid rain or storms.

Forests need to be well-managed if they are to grow as they should and provide wood for industry. This means thoughtful practices including weeding, pruning and replanting.

The area of tropical forests in the Amazon, Africa and Asia is shrinking every year. Why? Because trees are being cleared to build roads, provide wood for heating, and to make way for crops and grasslands. Thousands of living species (both plants and animals) disappear every year because of this.

Clearing the land results in 'desertification'. This means that the soil is of such poor quality, nothing can grow there any more. It can be due to a dry climate, but it can also be caused by human actions such as the felling of trees, increased farming or excessive pumping of underground water. When the farmable land disappears it takes a very long time to get it back.

What can we do?

How can we protect the environment? Every day we have to make an effort to do little things to care for our surroundings. We also need to learn more about nature so we can be more respectful of it. This means paying attention to what is happening around us and in the world.

'Big oaks from little acorns grow' – little things have a big impact. Everyone can take action in small ways. How? By using less water and not polluting it, not damaging the soil, and not putting toxic substances into the air. We can sort and recycle our rubbish, and buy products manufactured by processes that pollute less or not at all. By taking the bus you are polluting much less than driving in a car. A bicycle is even better. Thinking about these things is all part of protecting the environment.

Have you thought about the waste caused by buying water in plastic bottles?
There's making the bottles, transporting them long distances, and dealing with
the left-over plastic. Most plastic bottles end up at the dump.

You can learn about nature everywhere: in the city, the country, in parks and reserves,
with your family, on school trips, or with organisations that run nature camps.
And you can read, watch documentaries or visit science museums.

A large number of species are threatened with extinction today – fish, turtles, whales, tigers, parrots, monkeys, elephants, corals, and many insects. Scientists estimate that around 30,000 species disappear every year due to pollution, deforestation, hunting and fishing. Today it is illegal to trade 700 endangered species and there are strict regulations for 2,700 others.

The earth is a big place and can probably be home to a lot of people. But the population is skyrocketing, from two billion people in 1930, to six billion in 2000, and maybe double that by 2040. This means there are going to be some serious problems with water supply, food, health, energy use and pollution. How will the planet be able to cope?

Today we have the means to feed a large number of people. Well-planned agricultural systems and more co-operation between nations could make this happen. We need to act carefully, and think of non-polluting ways to promote long-term development.

Countries are now beginning to take action to protect the environment. It happens through the protection of species, anti-pollution regulations, the Antarctic Treaty and waste management agreements. Sadly, things are not equal between rich and poor countries – this has a serious impact on the environment. Poor countries are often pressured into using up their natural resources just to survive. This cannot continue.

Ecological associations working to protect the environment play a major role, because they are able to make people aware of serious issues. Let's save Earth!

Energy sources contained in the soil, such as coal, oil and natural gas, are non-renewable and will probably run out within the next few decades. Besides, they cause pollution and contribute to the greenhouse effect. Heat, light, water and wind are all renewable energy sources. Renewable means they will be available to us as long as the sun exists. Non-renewable or renewable – the choice is ours.

Eco-quiz

Now that you have learned about the environment and ecology, you can ask your friends and family some questions.

1. What are two elements that living things need in order to live?

2. Name two natural cycles that are important.

3. What is the soil made up of?

4. What is the difference between Earth and earth?

5. What are the two main substances plants feed on?

6. Plants can make their own food – true or false?

7. I am the waste produced by green plants. What am I called?

8. What name is given to this series of actions: the bird eats the insect that fed on the sap of the tree?

9. A cloud is made up of water vapour only – true or false?

10. Plants release a lot of water vapour into the air – true or false?

11. Water does not dissolve things easily – true or false?

12. How high is Mount Everest?

13. Without the greenhouse effect, the surface of the earth would be very hot – true or false?

14. The largest percentage of gas in the air is oxygen – true or false?

15. What does the ozone layer protect us from?

16. A European person uses less water than a person in Ghana – true or false?

17. How many people are killed each year by water-borne diseases — 1 million, 10 million, or 100 million?

18. It takes more water to produce a kilo of corn than a kilo of sugar — true or false?

19. A bath uses more than three times as much water as a shower — true or false?

20. DDT can end up in animals and humans. What is DDT?

21. What are the two main types of chemicals that farmers spread on their fields?

22. What do you call the invasion of waterways by overgrowth of algae or other plants?

23. Waste water is cleaned in the following order: Separation, Decanting, Biological treatment, Clarification, Screening. True or false?

24. Where is waste water cleaned?

25. Which sea has shrunk to half its size over the last fifty years? The Black Sea, the Aral Sea or the Caspian Sea?

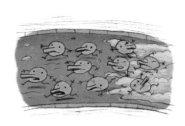

26. What is a toxic gas that attaches itself to red blood cells and prevents people from breathing?

27. A century from now, the sea will most likely have risen. How far?

28. What causes the increase of carbon dioxide (CO_2) in the air?

29. Is ozone a toxic gas?

30. What takes longer to break down: plastic bottles or tin cans?

31. Is it possible to heat buildings by burning rubbish?

32. Polar fleece can be manufactured from old water bottles — true or false?

33. What is a unit for measuring sound called?

34. In France, nuclear power makes up what percentage of the total energy produced: 25%, 50% or 75%?

35. What do the initials GMO mean?

36. Are coal and oil renewable energy sources?

37. How many people will there probably be on the earth in the year 2040?

38. How many species of animals disappear every year?

39. What is renewable energy?

40. Where are the biggest forests in the world?

Answers

1. Air and water.
2. The water cycle, the carbon cycle and others.
3. Soil is made up of sand, rock, clay, dead leaves, and decaying creatures.
4. Earth is the planet, and earth is the soil plants grow in.
5. Water and carbon dioxide.
6. True.
7. Oxygen.
8. A food chain.
9. False. It contains a lot of liquid water (and ice)
10. True. It's called evapotranspiration.
11. False. Water dissolves many things.
12. 8,848 metres.
13. False. It would be around -18°C on the surface of the earth.
14. False. It's mainly nitrogen.
15. It protects the earth from the sun's ultraviolet rays.
16. False. A European uses more water on average.
17. Around 10 million each year.
18. True.
19. True.
20. An insecticide chemical used in the past by farmers.
21. Chemical fertilisers and pesticides.
22. Eutrophication.
23. False. Screening is the first step.
24. A water treatment station or plant.
25. The Aral Sea.
26. Carbon monoxide.
27. It will rise about 50 cms or more.
28. Mostly the burning of oil and coal – in engines, heating systems and factories.
29. Ozone is a toxic gas when it is present in the air we breathe.
30. Plastic bottles.
31. Yes. In an incineration plant equipped with an energy recovery system.
32. True.
33. The decibel.
34. Approximately 75%.
35. Genetically Modified Organism.
36. Coal and oil are not renewable energy sources.
37. 10 to 12 billion.
38. 30,000 species.
39. It is a source of energy that cannot be exhausted, like the sun.
40. Canada, Siberia and the Amazon.

Eco-words

1. The study of how living things are connected to their surroundings is called _____.

2. The gas that makes up most of the air we breathe is _____.

3. Substances in the cell nucleus that decide the development of each individual.

4. Chemical that kills bugs — also called an insecticide.

5. A gas found in a very thin layer at about 30 to 40 kilometres high.

6. One of the important elements that living things need in order to live.

7. Unit of measurement for sound.

8. The main chemical element in living beings is _____.

1. To reduce rubbish we need to re-use and _____.

2. This dangerous stuff has very fine fibres which are used for insulating.

3. A man famous for his ideas about evolution.

4. Resources available to us as long as the sun exists are _____.

5. A gas made by plants which we need to live.

6. The layers of gases that surround Earth.

7. A power station that uses a controlled explosion to make electricity.

8. A reef where coral is endangered is the Great _____ Reef.

9. The gas form of water is called _____.

10. A green water plant that can invade waterways in masses.

11. A kind of transport that doesn't make pollution, and keeps you fit.

12. A drain that collects rainwater off streets is called _____.

13. When natural environments become poisoned or dirty, it is called _____.

Eco-dictionary

Acid rain
Rain in which acids (pollution) are dissolved from the air and come down in rainfall. Can cause serious damage, particularly to trees.

Atmosphere
The layers of gases that surround Earth.

Bio-indicators
Living creatures, such as trout, whose presence or absence indicates the degree of pollution of an area.

Biology
The science of life forms.

Carbon
The main chemical element in living beings.

Carbon dioxide
Gas (CO_2) produced by the respiration of living creatures and by combustion.

Combustion
Chemical reaction between a substance and oxygen. Combustion produces energy. Commonly called 'burning'.

Cycle
A series of stages through which a substance passes on the surface of the earth.

Decibel

Unit of measurement for sound. Sounds above 80 to 100 decibels can be harmful to human ears.

Desertification

Disappearance of vegetation and animal species. A result of climate change and lack of rainfall – sometimes speeded by human activity.

Dump, tip

Area where waste is stored. In well-managed dumps, the bottom of the storage area is lined and the run-off water is collected and treated.

Ecology

Science of the relationships of living beings with one another, and with the environments they inhabit.

Ecosystem

The interaction of living creatures – both plant and animal – and their natural environment, such as a forest or pond.

Evapotranspiration

The release of water into the atmosphere as a result of plant activity.

Fertilisers

Natural or chemical substances that are mixed into the soil to promote plant growth.

Genes

Substances coded in the cell nucleus of living things. Genes decide the development and functioning of each individual.

Greenhouse effect

Heating up of the lower layers of the atmosphere due to the presence of gases — including carbon dioxide, methane and water vapour.

Pesticide

Chemical spread over the soil and plants to kill or prevent the development of organisms harmful to plants. Also called insecticide.

Radioactivity

Property of certain substances which emit rays that can be dangerous to health, even fatal.

Recycling

Action of reusing an object, or the material it is made of, to avoid throwing it away. Recycling reduces consumption of primary materials and energy.

Species

Group of life forms sharing all their main characteristics and able to reproduce with one another.

Some useful websites

Ecology

www.ecokids.ca

www.epa.gov/kids

earth911.com

www.planetpatrol.info

www.eco-pros.com/ecologykids.htm

Water

www.waterfootprint.org

www.savewater.com.au

Recycling

www.reducerubbish.govt.nz

www.freecycle.org